Books by Roberta Pliner

The Lazy Indoor Gardener
Rx for Ailing House Plants (with Charles M. Evans)
The Terrarium Book (with Charles M. Evans)

The Lazy Indoor Gardener

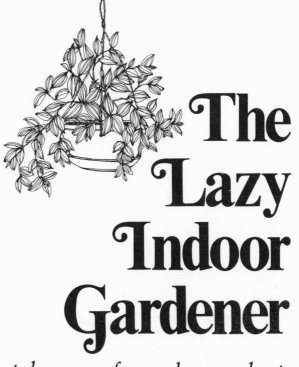

The Lazy Indoor Gardener

*How to take care of your house plants
with the least possible effort*

Roberta Pliner

Illustrations by Lilly Langotsky Kolker

Random House   New York

Acknowledgments

To the Edward Albee Foundation, Judith Antonelli, Roland Antonelli, Dr. Howard Lebwith and Charles Evans for assistance while writing this book and to Patrick Kenny's miserably neglected, ever-thriving Dracaena massangeanas for the inspiration for the book.

Library of Congress Cataloging in Publication Data
Pliner, Roberta Lee.
The lazy indoor gardener.
1. House plants. I. Title.
SB419.P58   635.9'65   75-37968
ISBN 0-394-49807-0
ISBN 0-394-73160-3 pbk.

Manufactured in the United States of America
98765432
First Edition

For Staten Island, where we made an art of being lazy

Contents

The Lazy Indoor Gardener

So You Want to Be a Lazy Gardener

T he perfect indoor plant is one that grows and thrives and blooms with no care whatever from its owner. It is the ideal solution to lazy indoor gardening except that, much as we all would like it, there is no such thing. Botanical science has yet to invent the instant house plant. On the other hand, the lazy gardener does not have to make a career of raising indoor plants. Whatever you've heard to the contrary, it's really not necessary to have a love affair with every leaf in order to have a beautiful house plant collection.

There are ways of indoor gardening that can keep the usual house-plant *grande passion* on the more casual level of platonic friendship. You can ignore some of the traditional plant no-no's, skip a lot of frills, turn off the Bach sonatas, and still have great plants.

Your best chance for a fairly care-free indoor garden lies in choosing plants that fit your home environment. Be sure you understand the limits of light, temperature, and humidity in your house or apartment. Then look for plants that can adapt to those conditions. This is the first and most important step toward ensuring a successful indoor garden with relatively little effort on your part.

The next step is selecting easy-care, not-too-fussy plants. Some plants—notably orchids, most ferns, miniature roses, bonsai plants, and all carnivorous plants—are temperamental prima donnas that should probably be cultivated only by people steeped in gardening lore with the time and inclination to become very involved with their greenery. Other plants—pothos, dracaena, prayer plant, Chinese evergreen, aspidistra, impatiens—are sweetly reasonable creatures that leaf and branch out freely, seldom attract insects, adapt to most growing conditions, and co-exist comfortably with the laziest gardener.

These are your plants if you're a busy gardener, a peripatetic gardener, or a just plain lazy gardener. If you think that any horticultural activity on your part beyond watering is too much, if other parts of your life leave you little time for plant care, if you travel frequently or commute between city and country homes and want plants in one place which can survive your departure to the other, then these reasonable plants are what you should look for and buy. Most are great for the fits-and-starts gardener, who hovers over the plants for several weeks or so at a time and then barely remembers to water them for months on end.

If you are a lazy or busy gardener, you've probably had to cope with the annoyance and expense of losing some good plants now and then, or even possibly all your plants. Cheer up—this book will help you work out some new strategies of lazy gardening. First read Chapter 2 on plant environment and apply the principles therein to your own home. Then refer to Chapter 3 for descriptions of plants best suited to lazy gardening and other plants to be avoided by a lazy gardener. If you compare the environmental requirements of individual plants with what you know about the environment of your own home, then you should get a general idea of which plants to look for. Check Chapter 4 for tips on where and how to shop for plants. Once you've brought your new treasures home, follow the simple directions for routine and occasional plant care in Chapters 5 and 6. Chapter 7 is a compendium of further strategies for easy, lazy gardening.

2

The Plant's Environment

Most house plants manage with indoor growing conditions—light, humidity, air, and temperature—that are somewhat less than perfect. This is just as well, because if conditions were too perfect, the plants would literally crowd you out of your own home. In their original habitats many modest-sized house plants are massive vines and immense trees. Even so, any plant is more likely to live and be well if its indoor environment somewhat approximates that of its native jungle or wherever it comes from.

How do you accomplish this? Either you alter conditions to suit the plant, or you choose plants to suit existing conditions. The latter course is much to be preferred for lazy gardening, but it means that you have to define those conditions before bringing home new plants.

While you are learning to define your home environment, keep in mind your own limitations. Just how much (or how little) effort are you willing to spend in taking care of the plants? If a plant requires a cool room in winter and a warm room in summer but your idea of seasonal comfort is having the radiator turned on full in winter and the air conditioner set on high in summer, then that plant is not your plant. If a plant has to be mist-sprayed every day because its survival depends on very high humidity, you probably don't want that plant either.

light Of all the elements that support and encourage healthy plants, the light is the most important. Not enough of it is the most common reason why so many frustrated gardeners exclaim "I can't grow anything." Everyone can grow something—it's a matter of understanding just how much light you really have and finding plants that will grow in that much light.

If a plant looks extremely leggy, with its leaves set much farther apart than seems normal, and its color is wrong, or if all your plants regularly collapse after a month or two in your home no matter what kind of care you give them, insufficient light is almost certainly the problem. If plant leaves are scorched or shriveled and plants are dry and wilted even though the soil in the pots is still damp, it could be that the plants are receiving too much light, especially if they are set in windows that are lit by hot afternoon sun.

Plant light is usually assessed in levels of high, medium, and low. High light is what plants receive in windows facing south into which the sun shines for most of the day. Medium light is available in windows that face east or west, where the sun hits them either in the morning or afternoon. Low light occurs in windows that face north, where the sun doesn't shine at all. Low light is daylight without sun.

The length of day and the number of hours of the day that the sun shines into any window also determine the light available to plants. Daylength in most places is about nine hours in winter and fourteen hours in summer. Although the sun may shine into a window for the same amount of time in both in winter and summer, in winter the sun is low on the horizon and the intensity of sunlight will be less than in summer.

However, these assessments assume completely unobstructed windows, which quite often is not the case. Trees, shrubbery, nearby buildings, a wing on one side of a house, dark curtains or shutters, and high levels of air pollution can reduce the available light or the intensity of light in any window. You can't judge the light level in your windows simply by knowing which direction they face.

To illustrate: In my first apartment, I had huge windows facing north, but the next building was so close (about four feet away) that I had to call the weather service every morning to find out whether I needed a raincoat to go to work. What might have been very good daylight for low-light plants turned out to be no light at all; I was living in an air shaft.

The windows in my next apartment faced south across the street from a tunnel entrance. Because the nearest buildings were two blocks away and I was on the fourth floor just above the treetops, the sun poured in all day and flooded the whole place with light. It was a houseplant gardener's dream: unblocked southern exposure. I grew a jungle in that apartment.

I now live in a backyard apartment. Most of my windows face south, and theoretically I should be able to grow another jungle. However, the apartment is on the ground floor, and the backs of the buildings on the next block cut down the light. Moreover, the biggest windows are set into an alcove formed by the rear wings of my building and the building next door. Instead of having sun most of the day, as is characteristic of south windows, the plants receive sunlight for just two or three hours.

Since these conditions produce medium light, I collected some medium-light plants—of the most effortless variety, of course. They did pretty well during the first winter, and I looked forward to the longer days of spring and summer when I thought they would do even better. What I hadn't anticipated was that five straggly trees in my backyard, which I thought were dead, leafed out and bloomed in great abundance during the summer. The yard is so heavily shaded that my windows get no sun at all! During the height of the growing season when plants most need light, the light for all my plants is low at best.

The Lazy Indoor Gardener

After my plants responded to their reduced light level by shedding half their leaves, I moved them out to the backyard, where the sun pokes in now and then between the trees. And I lie in a hammock on hot days in the shade of the obstructive trees and make lists of low-light plants to buy!

Obviously, available plant light varies with each individual situation. The most accurate and easiest way to measure light levels in your windows is to use a photographic light meter, the incident reading type, which measures the light falling on the subject, in this case the plants. (The built-in exposure meter on some cameras, if it is the direct reading type, can also be used to measure plant light.) Focus the light meter on the area where you want to put the plants. Set the ASA film speed at 400 and the shutter speed at 1/125 of a second. The *f* stop (lens opening) will indicate your light level.

$$f\,4 = \text{low light}$$
$$f\,5.6 = \text{medium light}$$
$$f\,8 - f\,11 = \text{high light}$$

Most plants can adjust to somewhat higher rather than lower light levels, so if you get an in-between reading, figure the light level as equivalent to the lower reading. Take your readings on a bright day when the sun is high over the horizon. Be sure not to focus the meter on the shadow of your hand or nearby objects.

If you don't have a light meter, you can assess the light levels in plant windows by observing, on a sunny day, which windows receive sunlight and for how many hours of the day.

4 or more hours of sun = high light
2–3 hours of sun, bright daylight remainder of day = medium light
1 hour or less of sun = low light

High indoor light is equivalent to bright light without sun outdoors. Low light can be too low to support plant growth, but if you can read newsprint comfortably near windows that receive little or no sun, then plants will survive in those windows.

If your windows are large or unobstructed, you might find that the interior of the room is quite bright and sunlit for part of the day at distances as far as five to ten feet from a window. In most cases, however, you can safely assume that the light level is reduced at any point farther than three feet from a window. If the window is recessed, the light level is reduced in areas farther than eighteen inches from it. If you want to grow plants away from the windows of a bright room, rotate the plants weekly so that each has a chance to benefit from the best available light. Alternatively, you can use high- or medium-light plants in the window and low-light plants away from the window.

artificial light

If you determine that you have less than low light in any window, then that window is a plant no-no. Unless there are better locations, you will have to use artificial light.

Admittedly, it's a nuisance to set up lights just for plants, but if window light is hopeless for *any* plant or if you want plants that require higher light levels than what you have, you really have no other choice.

For artificial light to work as a substitute for sun, the lights have to run the gamut of the color spectrum from red to blue. Incandescent lights (most ordinary light bulbs) are too high at the red end of the spectrum, although you can use them to supplement borderline natural light. The so-called grow lamps that you'll see around for about five to seven dollars are incandescent flood lamps. For about a third of the cost, you can use photographic flood lamps, which are the same thing without the fancy packaging.

The simplest effective artificial plant light is the Duro-

Test Fluomeric, a color-balanced mercury vapor lamp. It is a flood lamp—an expensive one—that combines certain features of fluorescent and incandescent lighting to produce a perfectly balanced light source for most plants. You can buy just the bulb at plant and some electrical fixture stores and screw it into any flood-lamp fixture, or you can buy it with its own simple, rather attractive fixture. It can be set on a table or, better, mounted on a wall or ceiling pointing toward the window at such an angle that it focuses on as much of the plants as possible. Since this is a hot light (250 watts), it should be set about five to seven feet from the plants.

There you have it. One simple flood lamp solves all your light problems. It will even cover a fairly large growing area—about three or four square feet. There's just one catch. The bulb costs about $50 and with the fixture it comes to about $100. However, if you have a couple of hundred dollars or so invested in plants that will not survive without proper light, it might be worth it. The bulb comes with a two-year guarantee, which makes the cost slightly more palatable. If it's any comfort, the wholesale cost isn't much less.

For somewhat less money, cool white, daylight, or plant-growing fluorescent lights can boost window light considerably. Mount fluorescent fixtures vertically along the window frame, and if you have tall plants or hanging plants, horizontally at the top of the window frame. Fluorescent tubes come in various lengths and wattages ranging from eighteen-inch tubes of 15 watts to forty-eight-inch tubes of 40 watts. The higher the wattage and the closer the plants are to the lights, the greater the light level. Plants placed in the center of the window sill should be rotated with those at the sides every week or so, in order that all plants have a chance to be near the lights. Fluorescent tubes are cool lights, and plants can be as close as three inches from them. If your curtains or shutters conceal the lights from the interior of the room, you might be able to save a little on cost by not buying the reflectors that go with the fixtures.

Fluorescent tubes and mercury-vapor lamps can be used as the only light source for plants in places where there is no window light. However, fluorescent tubes mounted in the window are obviously not helpful for lighting floor plants. For these plants you really need the mercury-vapor lamps because they can be mounted on the ceiling or high up on a wall. Whichever you use, be sure the lights are turned off when you go to bed. Plants need about eight hours or so of darkness every day. If you hook up the lights to a timer, you don't have to think about when to turn them off and on.

Humidity is the moisture in the air without which neither plants nor people can survive. In most homes, it ranges from poor to terrible. The humidity in any desert is better. Central heating is the culprit, because it produces hot, dry air. That's why plants often shrivel up and die in winter when indoor heat is high, even though all other conditions are good. Lack of humidity also causes distorted and stunted plant growth, or it may stop growth altogether. **humidity**

If plants that are well watered look dried out and wrinkly, if leaf edges are brown and shriveled up, if your hair and skin are dry and lusterless and you wake up every morning feeling as if you can hardly breathe, you can be sure that the humidity in your home is extremely low and unhealthy for you as well as your plants. A gadget called a hygrometer (about $5 and up in hardware and department stores) measures humidity the way thermometers measure temperature. Fifty percent would be an ideal indoor humidity, but you and the plants could get along well in a range of 30 to 40 percent.

The only places where indoor humidity naturally occurs at reasonably healthy levels for plants and people is at the seacoast or in heavily wooded areas where the air is nearly always damp. During a rainy spell, particularly in mild weather when windows are open, indoor humidity anywhere might be fairly high.

What do you do about low humidity? The simplest and best device—and, as usual, the most expensive—is a humidifier. Quite aside from the benefits to your plants, the use of a humidifier is a particularly good idea for you if dry, overheated air is a constant problem.

Less effective but also less expensive ways to raise humidity are to keep thermostat or radiator controls as low as you can stand it; to cluster plants in one place (they raise the humidity for each other in the growing area); or to stand plants on trays of pebbles and water. The depth of the pebbles (or sand or bricks or gravel) should be high enough so that the pots stand above the water line.

If you live alone or even if you don't, leaving the bathroom door open when you take a shower raises the humidity in rooms near the bathroom (you can see moisture condensing on window panes). Mist-spraying as often as possible is very helpful to plants in dry, hot rooms. Most of the plants in Chapter 3 do not require very high humidity, but all benefit from higher humidity than is likely to occur in the average home.

temperature Most plants, and certainly all the plants in this book, will survive and grow nicely at the normal room temperature range of 68 to 72 degrees. In summer, if your plants receive afternoon sun, which is particularly hot, you might have to move them away from the window. In winter, areas near or on top of any heating unit or near incandescent lights will be hotter than the rest of the room. If the top of the radiator is the only place to put the plants (because the only decent light comes from the window over the radiator), set them on trays of pebbles and water. This method doesn't lower the temperature, but raises the humidity so that plants don't wilt from the extra warm, dry air. You might try putting some kind of shelf over the radiator that juts out past it by several inches or so and deflects the heat outward toward the center of the room instead of upward toward the plants. It's also a good idea to lower the thermostat or radiator controls at night. Plants grow better if the temperature is dropped at night by five or ten degrees.

Cool temperatures are not usually an issue except when plants spend cold winters in completely unheated houses (such as vacation homes). Few plants suffer from being near drafty windows or from touching cold windowpanes (if anything, they benefit from the draft because it reduces the temperature in windows over the radiator). But if winters in your locality are harsh, ice-coated windows might cause plants to shrivel up and die.

Like you, your plants benefit from a daily dose of fresh air. **air** In extremely cold weather you should open windows other than those in which the plants are sitting. On normally cold days a mild breeze will do no harm to most plants.

Air conditioning is perfectly safe for plants as long as they are not in the direct line of a blast of cold air. In fact, air conditioning is good for plants because it provides air circulation and ventilation in what might otherwise be hot, closed rooms.

3
The Lazy Gardener's Plants

Having figured out what environmental conditions exist in your home, you can now begin to match plants to those conditions.

Here are three lists of plants. The first covers easily grown, readily available plants that are not too fussy about growing conditions. The second list describes plants that are also easily grown, providing certain environmental conditions are just right. Either the light must be especially good, or the plant needs special care, as described under "Characteristics." The third list includes plants you should not buy if your gardening is to be a maximum-result, minimum-effort affair.

Except where noted otherwise, all plants on the first two lists can live in relatively low humidity, but all would benefit from a range of 30 to 40 percent. Soil, watering, and light requirements are indicated for each plant. If a range of conditions is given (for example, moderate to heavy watering), you can choose, but that choice should be permanent for the plant's benefit. If it ever becomes necessary to alter a plant's growing environment, make the change very gradually.

Without exception and with no great effort, the plants on the first two lists usually prosper for lazy gardeners despite the most erratic attentions or inattentions, the vagaries of heating systems, and the unpredictable factors in the day-to-day existence of all living things. Note which plants suit you and your home, and choose from these when you shop for new plants.

Very reasonable plants

AGLAONEMA spp. (Chinese evergreen)
    LIGHT: low to medium
    SOIL: humus
    WATERING: heavy
    LOCATION: window sill
    CHARACTERISTICS: tall and elongated solid light-green or mottled green leaves

ASPIDISTRA ELATIOR (cast-iron plant)
    LIGHT: any exposure
    SOIL: all-purpose
    WATERING: moderate
    LOCATION: window sill
    CHARACTERISTICS: tall; dark-green broad leaves growing from a single base

CEROPEGIA WOODII (rosary vine, string-of-hearts)

    LIGHT: any exposure

    SOIL: sandy

    WATERING: moderate

    LOCATION: hanging pot

    CHARACTERISTICS: small-leaved vine; purplish color with tiny flowers if grown in high light; mottled green in lower light; new plants grow from small bulbs along the stems that can be set half in, half out of the soil

CHLOROPHYTUM COMOSUM (spider plant)

    LIGHT: low to medium

    SOIL: sandy

    WATERING: light

    LOCATION: hanging pot

    CHARACTERISTICS: solid green or green-and-white grassy leaves; long runners produce little plantlets that can be set in soil for new plants

C. rhombifolia

CISSUS spp. (C. RHOMBIFOLIA, grape ivy; **C. ANTARCTICA,** kangaroo vine)

LIGHT: any exposure

SOIL: all-purpose

WATERING: moderate

LOCATION: hanging pot

CHARACTERISTICS: climbing vine; saw-toothed, medium-size green leaves; trains easily on stakes or up strings around the window

C. antarctica

DIEFFENBACHIA spp. (dumb cane)

LIGHT: low to medium

SOIL: all-purpose

WATERING: moderate

LOCATION: window sill

CHARACTERISTICS: variegated tall leaves; causes slight form of lock-jaw if eaten; fast-growing

DRACAENA spp. (D. MASSANGEANA, corn plant; **D. MARGINATA; D. SANDERIANA,** ribbon plant; **D. GODSEFFIANA,** gold dust plant; **D. DEREMENSIS 'WARNECKII')**

LIGHT: any exposure

SOIL: all-purpose

WATERING: light

LOCATION: floor

CHARACTERISTICS: elongated striped leaves growing in clusters on top of single trunk; *D. marginata* branches out; all give palm-tree effect; extremely durable

D. massangeana

D. deremensis 'Warneckii'

D. sanderiana

D. marginata

D. godseffiana

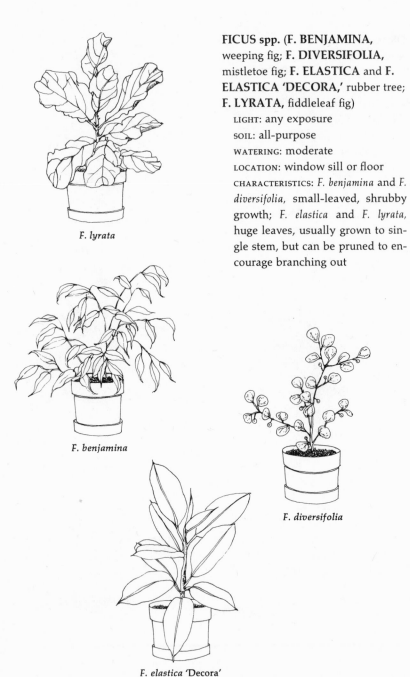

F. lyrata

F. benjamina

F. diversifolia

F. elastica 'Decora'

FICUS spp. (F. BENJAMINA, weeping fig; **F. DIVERSIFOLIA,** mistletoe fig; **F. ELASTICA** and **F. ELASTICA 'DECORA,'** rubber tree; **F. LYRATA,** fiddleleaf fig)

LIGHT: any exposure

SOIL: all-purpose

WATERING: moderate

LOCATION: window sill or floor

CHARACTERISTICS: *F. benjamina* and *F. diversifolia*, small-leaved, shrubby growth; *F. elastica* and *F. lyrata*, huge leaves, usually grown to single stem, but can be pruned to encourage branching out

GREVILLEA ROBUSTA (silk oak)
LIGHT: medium
SOIL: all-purpose
WATERING: moderate
LOCATION: floor
CHARACTERISTICS: lacy, symmetrical branches, silvery green; easily grown from seed

HYPOESTES SANGUINOLENTA
(polka-dot plant, measles plant)
LIGHT: medium
SOIL: humus
WATERING: heavy
LOCATION: window sill
CHARACTERISTICS: shrubby oval leaves, green with pink polka dots; prune to keep bushy

LIGUSTRUM JAPONICUM
'TEXANUM' (Japanese privet)
LIGHT: low to medium
SOIL: all-purpose
WATERING: moderate
LOCATION: floor
CHARACTERISTICS: freely branching, small, leathery, dark-green leaves

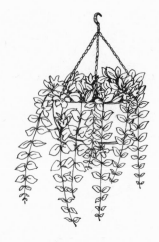

LYSIMACHIA NUMMULARIA
(moneywort)
   LIGHT: low
   SOIL: all-purpose
   WATERING: moderate
   LOCATION: hanging pot
   CHARACTERISTICS: small rounded, dark green leaves on long runners

MARANTA LEUCONEURA
(prayer plant)
   LIGHT: low to medium
   SOIL: all-purpose
   WATERING: moderate
   LOCATION: window sill
   CHARACTERISTICS: large oval leaves veined red with silver centers or spotted dark-green or brown, which fold up at night like praying hands (to conserve moisture) and open during the day

PALMS (CHAMAEDOREA spp., including **C. ELEGANS,** neanthe bella palm; **HOWEIA spp.,** the palm court palms; **PHOENIX spp.,** including **P. ROEBELENII,** date palm, **RHAPIS spp.,** lady palm)

    LIGHT: low to medium
    SOIL: all-purpose
    WATERING: heavy
    LOCATION: large window sill or floor tree
    CHARACTERISTICS: clustering, grassy leaves; some single-stemmed, some multibranched

C. elegans

Chamaedorea sp.

Howeia sp.

Phoenix sp.

PANDANUS VEITCHI
(screw-pine)
LIGHT: medium
SOIL: all-purpose
WATERING: moderate in summer;
light in winter
LOCATION: window sill
CHARACTERISTICS: long, spiky leaves
banded in silver on single stalk

PEPEROMIA spp. (P. CAPERATA
'Emerald Ripple'; **P. SANDERSII,**
watermelon peperomia; and others)
LIGHT: low to medium
SOIL: all-purpose or sandy
WATERING: light
LOCATION: window sill
CHARACTERISTICS: low-growing,
round leaves in various colors and
textures; most are semisucculent

P. caperata 'Emerald Ripple'

P. sandersii

PILEA spp. (P. CADIEREI, aluminum plant; **P. 'SILVER TREE';** **P. INVOLUCRATA,** sometimes called seersucker plant)

LIGHT: medium to high (for varie-gated colors)

SOIL: all-purpose

WATERING: light

LOCATION: window sill

CHARACTERISTICS: low-growing, bushy, with small, rounded leaves in variety of colors, some heavily textured; avoid *P. depressa,* baby's tears, and *P. microphylla,* artillery plant)

P. cadierei

P. involucrata

P. 'Silver Tree'

P. Selloum

P. oxycardium

P. pertusum

PHILODENDRON spp. (P. OXYCARDIUM, common heart-leaf philodendron; **P. PERTUSUM,** split-leaf philodendron; **P. SELLOUM; P. PANDURA FORMAE,** fiddle-leaf philodendron; **P. RADIATUM,** similar to but more graceful than split-leaf; **P. MELANOCHRYSON,** velvet-leaf philodenron)

LIGHT: any exposure

SOIL: all-purpose

WATERING: moderate

LOCATION: window sill or floor if trained on supports

CHARACTERISTICS: most are large-leaved shrubs or heavy vines requiring supports; *P. melanochryson* and *P. oxycardium,* small-leaved vines for hanging baskets which should be pruned frequently for bushy growth

P. pandura formae

Philodendron sp.

PLECTRANTHUS spp. (P. AUSTRALIS, Swedish ivy; **P. COLEOIDES 'MARGINATUS')**

    LIGHT: low to medium

    SOIL: all-purpose

    WATERING: moderate

    LOCATION: hanging pot

    CHARACTERISTICS: hanging basket; fast-growing semisucculent, dark-green round leaves; P. *'Marginatus'* leaves edged in white; large plants produce scented flowers in good light

P. australis

P. coleoides 'Marginatus'

PODOCARPUS MACROPHYLLUS (yew pine)

    LIGHT: low to medium

    SOIL: all-purpose

    WATERING: moderate

    LOCATION: floor

    CHARACTERISTICS: leathery, small, dark-green oval leaves, shrubby growth

RHEO DISCOLOR
(Moses-in-the-cradle)
 LIGHT: any exposure
 SOIL: all-purpose
 WATERING: light or moderate
 LOCATION: window sill
 CHARACTERISTICS: spearlike stiff leaves on single stalk, flowers grow in cups at base of leaves

SANSEVIERIA spp. (snake plant)
 LIGHT: any exposure
 SOIL: all-purpose or sandy
 WATERING: light
 LOCATION: window sill
 CHARACTERISTICS: tall, spiky, mottled leaves edged in yellow, most nearly indestructible plant; *S. 'Hahnii'* is short-leaved variety

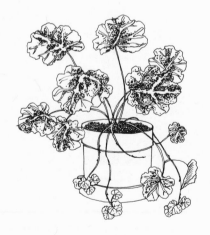

SAXIFRAGA SARMENTOSA
(strawberry begonia)
 LIGHT: low to medium (flowers in higher light)
 SOIL: all-purpose
 WATERING: moderate
 LOCATION: window sill or hanging pot
 CHARACTERISTICS: round, fuzzy leaves with long runners producing little plantlets that can be set in new pots and rooted; variety *'Tricolor'* has pink, white, and green leaves if grown in good light

SCHEFFLERA ACTINOPHYLLA
(umbrella tree)
  LIGHT: medium
  SOIL: all-purpose
  WATERING: moderate
  LOCATION: floor
  CHARACTERISTICS: shrubby growth,
  shiny long oval leaves grow in cir-
  cles on long branches

SCINDAPSUS AUREUS (devil's
ivy, pothos)
  LIGHT: low to medium
  SOIL: all-purpose
  WATERING: moderate
  LOCATION: hanging pot
  CHARACTERISTICS: leathery leaves
  splotched in white or yellow; trails
  or climbs; resembles heart-leaf
  philodendron

SYNGONIUM PODOPHYLLUM
(arrow-head plant)
  LIGHT: any exposure
  SOIL: all-purpose
  WATERING: moderate
  LOCATION: window sill or hanging
  pot
  CHARACTERISTICS: moderately large
  arrow-shaped leaves, dark or light
  green and prominently veined; can
  be trained on supports or allowed
  to trail; prune for bushiness; fast-
  growing in good light

TETRASTIGMA VOINIERIANUM
(lizard plant, chestnut vine)
LIGHT: medium
SOIL: humus
WATERING: heavy
LOCATION: window sill or floor if trained on supports
CHARACTERISTICS: large, dusty-looking leaves; strong, vigorous climbing vine, trains itself against any support

TRADESCANTIA FLUMINENSIS and T.F. 'VARIEGATA' (wandering Jew)
LIGHT: any exposure
SOIL: all-purpose
WATERING: moderate
LOCATION: hanging pot
CHARACTERISTICS: pointed, green-and-purple or green-and-white thin waxy leaves on brittle stems; flowers in good light

ZEBRINA PENDULA (wandering jew, purple queen)
LIGHT: medium
SOIL: all-purpose
WATERING: moderate
LOCATION: hanging pot
CHARACTERISTICS: purple leaves slightly larger and like those of *Tradescantia* spp.; small pink and white flowers; plants usually last only a year or so, take cuttings and start new plants when old ones begin to droop and lose leaves

Reasonable plants on one condition

ABUTILON HYBRIDUM

(flowering maple)
LIGHT: high
SOIL: all-purpose
WATERING: heavy
LOCATION: hanging pot, window sill
or floor
CHARACTERISTICS: bell-shaped flow-
ers in red, white, and pink; maple-
like leaves; needs very good light
to flower

APHELANDRA SQUARROSA
'LOUISIAE' (zebra plant)
LIGHT: high
SOIL: all-purpose
WATERING: moderate
LOCATION: window sill
CHARACTERISTICS: compact plant
with large waxy green leaves
veined in white and yellow flower
clusters, needs extra good humid-
ity

A. densiflorus 'Sprengeri'

ASPARAGUS DENSIFLORUS 'SPRENGERI' and A. PLUMOSUS
(asparagus ferns)

LIGHT: good low to medium (full sun burns)

SOIL: humus

WATERING: moderate to heavy

LOCATION: hanging pot; window sill when very small

CHARACTERISTICS: masses of ferny foliage spilling out of baskets; if grown in daylight without sun, should be very bright daylight; watering very regular

A. plumosus

ARALIA spp. (DIZYGOTHECA ELEGANTISSIMA, false aralia; **POLYSCIAS FUTICOSA 'ELEGANS,'** Ming tree)

LIGHT: medium

SOIL: all-purpose

WATERING: moderate

LOCATION: floor or window sill if small

CHARACTERISTICS: false aralia has long, thin, notched leaves; watering must be regular, light good, and humidity better than average; Ming tree has curly, lacy leaves, responds well to being summered outdoors and allowed to go dormant for part of the winter (reduce watering, let leaves drop, increase watering when new growth starts)

Dizygotheca elegantissima

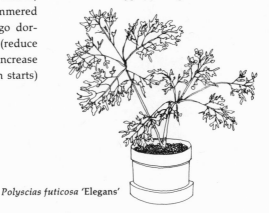

Polyscias futicosa 'Elegans'

ARDISIA CRISPA (coral berry)

LIGHT: medium

SOIL: all-purpose

WATERING: moderate

LOCATION: window sill

CHARACTERISTICS: waxy, dark-green long oval leaves, white flowers in spring, red berries in fall, needs slightly higher humidity than average

BEGONIA REX-CULTORUM (rex begonia)

LIGHT: medium

SOIL: humus

WATERING: moderate

LOCATION: window sill or hanging pot

CHARACTERISTICS: some varieties good for shallow hanging baskets; many brilliantly colored varieties and shapes, low-growing, flower spikes in spring; needs regular watering, preferably morning sun

BILLBERGIA spp. (bromeliad)

LIGHT: medium

SOIL: sandy

WATERING: heavy while growing; light in winter

LOCATION: window sill

CHARACTERISTICS: tall, stiff leaves growing in rosette fashion, flower spikes on tall, thin stems; cup formed by leaves must be kept filled with water as well as soil

BULBS—hyacinth, French Roman hyacinth, paperwhite narcissus

LIGHT: medium to high while growing, low after flowers appear

SOIL: water or water and pebbles (see below)

WATERING: constant level (see below)

LOCATION: window sill

HOW TO GROW: To force spring bulbs: put hyacinth bulbs in hyacinth glasses; nest narcissus and French Roman hyacinth bulbs (three or more) in a three- or four-

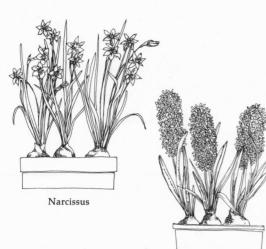

Narcissus

Hyacinth

inch layer of gravel or smooth pebbles in any watertight container and fill with water up to the base of bulbs and keep water level constant; cover bulbs with newspaper (with holes for ventilation) and set in cool place until roots form and tops sprout. Place in light window until flowers form, then in low light. Discard after flowering.

CACTI and other succulents
LIGHT: high
SOIL: sandy
WATERING: light
LOCATION: window sill, hanging basket, floor
CHARACTERISTICS: many types are easily grown if light is very good; many flower if kept cool (between 45 and 55 degrees) in winter and water is given just often enough to prevent shriveling; good species include *Aporocactus flagelliformis,* rat-tail cactus; mammillarias; euphorbias, including *E. splendens,* Christ-thorn; opuntias; notocacti; kalanchoes; sempervivums, hen-and-chickens; lithops, living stones; aloes; sedums; agaves; crassulas, including *C. argentea,* jade plant

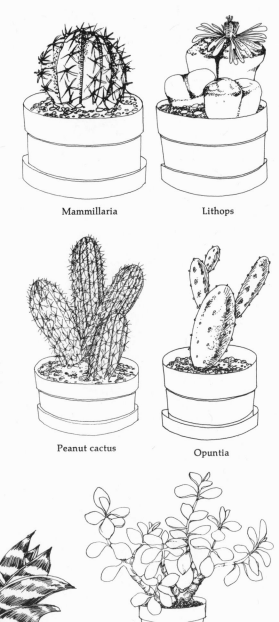

Mammillaria

Lithops

Peanut cactus

Opuntia

Jade plant

Aloe

CLERODENDRUM THOMSONAE (glorybower)

LIGHT: medium to high

SOIL: all-purpose

WATERING: heavy while budding and flowering; moderate otherwise

LOCATION: window sill or hanging basket

CHARACTERISTICS: heavy vine for climbing on support or hanging basket; oval dark-green leaves, flowers like Chinese lanterns; light must be good for flowering

CLIVIA MINIATA (Kaffir lily)

LIGHT: medium

SOIL: humus

WATERING: moderate

LOCATION: window sill

CHARACTERISTICS: tall, leathery, wide-bladed leaves, with cluster of bright orange flowers on tall stalk; roots should be very crowded in pot for flowering, so repotting every two or three years is sufficient

COLEUS BLUMEI (painted nettle)

LIGHT: high

SOIL: all-purpose

WATERING: moderate

LOCATION: window sill

CHARACTERISTICS: many brilliantly colored varieties in moderately large, differently shaped leaves; light must be high to hold color; extremely easy to grow from seed; droops after one year, so take cuttings and throw out old plant

CORDYLINE TERMINALIS (ti plant)
    LIGHT: medium to high
    SOIL: all-purpose
    WATERING: heavy while growing; moderate otherwise
    LOCATION: window sill
    CHARACTERISTICS: tall, thin red and yellow leaves, needs above-average humidity

FATSHEDERA LIZEI (ivy tree)
    LIGHT: medium
    SOIL: all-purpose
    WATERING: moderate
    LOCATION: window sill
    CHARACTERISTICS: shrubby, large ivylike leaves, requires somewhat cooler than average temperatures

FICUS PUMILA (creeping fig)
    LIGHT: low to medium
    SOIL: all-purpose
    WATERING: heavy
    LOCATION: hanging pot
    CHARACTERISTICS: trailing or climbing very small-leaved vine, freely branching; needs higher humidity than average, watering must be regular, frequent misting is very good

Saintpaulia ionantha

GESNERIADS (SAINTPAULIA IONANTHA, African violet, and **EPISCIA spp.,** flame violet)

LIGHT: low

SOIL: African violet potting mix

WATERING: moderate

LOCATION: window sill

CHARACTERISTICS: African violet—low-growing, with round, fuzzy leaves, white, pink, violet flowers; *Episcia* spp., larger leaves and red or yellow flowers, sometimes trails; do not mist or get water on leaves

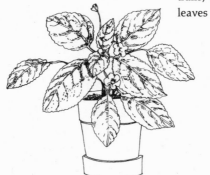

Episcia sp.

GYNURA AURANTIACA (velvet plant)

LIGHT: medium to high

SOIL: all-purpose

WATERING: heavy

LOCATION: hanging pot

CHARACTERISTICS: notched, elongated green leaves heavily coated with purple hairs; needs above average humidity; pick off flower buds

HEDERA HELIX var. (ivy)

LIGHT: low to medium
SOIL: all-purpose
WATERING: moderate
LOCATION: hanging basket, window sill
CHARACTERISTICS: trailing or climbing vines; wide variety of leaf shapes; small-leaved varieties usually most sturdy; need cooler temperatures, higher humidity than average; subject to spider mite if grown in hot, dry air

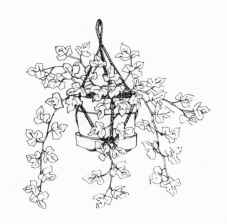

HOYA spp. (wax plant)

LIGHT: medium to high (less in winter)
SOIL: all-purpose
WATERING: light in winter, moderate while growing and flowering
LOCATION: hanging basket, window sill
CHARACTERISTICS: vine that trails or climbs with thick, waxy leaves, clusters of pink-and-white scented flowers in summer

IMPATIENS spp. (patience plant)

LIGHT: any exposurre
SOIL: all-purpose
WATERING: moderate
LOCATION: window sill
CHARACTERISTICS: bushy dark-green leaves, white, pink, orange, yellow, red flowers; needs some sun for flowering; plants last only a year or less, so take cuttings and discard old plants

IRESINE HERBSTII (blood-leaf)
   LIGHT: high
   SOIL: all-purpose
   WATERING: moderate
   LOCATION: window sill
   CHARACTERISTICS: red and reddish-yellow rounded leaves, bushy growth if pruned now and then

MYRTUS COMMUNIS MICROPHYLLA (myrtle)
   LIGHT: medium to high
   SOIL: humus
   WATERING: moderate
   LOCATION: window sill
   CHARACTERISTICS: bushy, tiny-leaved shrub; needs misting two or three times a week

NEPHROLEPSIS spp. (N. EXALTATA, 'BOSTONIENSE,' Boston fern; **N. E. 'ROOSEVELTII';** **N. E. 'FLUFFY RUFFLES')**

LIGHT: low

SOIL: humus

WATERING: heavy

LOCATION: window sill or hanging pot

CHARACTERISTICS: massive spreading ferns, easier and sturdier than other ferns; misting every two days is very beneficial

Boston Fern

Fluffy Ruffles

PITTOSPORUM TOBIRA

LIGHT: medium

SOIL: all-purpose

WATERING: heavy

LOCATION: floor

CHARACTERISTICS: needs sun for spring flowers; thick, leathery leaves circled around short branches, shrubby growth; should be grown in slightly cooler and more humid conditions than average

PUNICA GRANATUM 'NANA'
(dwarf pomegranate)
  LIGHT: high
  SOIL: all-purpose
  WATERING: moderate
  LOCATION: window sill
  CHARACTERISTICS: shrubby, glossy
  leaves, red flowers, edible fruit;
  may lose leaves occasionally

SENECIO MIKANIOIDES
(German ivy)
  LIGHT: medium to high
  SOIL: all-purpose
  WATERING: moderate
  LOCATION: hanging pot
  CHARACTERISTICS: ivy-shaped waxy
  leaves; small, yellow flowers in
  winter; light must be very good

SPATHIPHYLLUM spp. (spathe
flower)
  LIGHT: low to medium
  SOIL: humus
  WATERING: heavy
  LOCATION: window sill
  CHARACTERISTICS: large dark-green,
  floppy leaves on tall stalks, with
  white flowers like calla lilies; with
  proper humidity, plants bloom re-
  peatedly

TOLMIEA MENZIESII
(pick-a-back plant)
LIGHT: low to medium
SOIL: all-purpose
WATERING: heavy
LOCATION: window sill
CHARACTERISTICS: low-growing,
large, fuzzy green leaves with little
plantlets in centers; watering must
be regular and plant never allowed
to completely dry out

Plants not to buy

This list could be endless; there are innumerable plants
that are not good projects for lazy gardeners. The following are some commonly available plants that either require
meticulous attention to cultivation or have demanding
growing conditions.

Aeschynanthus spp. (lipstick vine)
Ananas spp. (pineapple)
Anthurium spp.
Araucaria heterophylla (Norfolk Island pine)
Azalea spp.
Bamboos and related grass plants
Begonia spp., except for *Begonia rex*
Beloperone guttata (shrimp plant)
Bougainvillea var.
Bromeliads, except for *Billbergia* spp.
Camellia japonica
Caladium bicolor

Carnivorous plants, such as *Darlingtonia californica.* (cobra
  lily), *Dionaea muscipula* (Venus fly-trap)
Cestrum spp. (Jessamine)
Columnea spp.
Crossandra infundibuliformis
Ferns, except *Nephrolepsis* spp.
Fuchsia spp.
Gardenia jasminoides
Herbs
Hibiscus rosa-sinensis
Lantana spp.
Malpighia coccigera (miniature holly)
Mimosa pudica (sensitive plant)
Nertera depressa (bead plant)
Orchid var.
Oxalis spp. (clover relatives)
Pelargonium spp. (geraniums)
Rosa chinensis 'Minima' and other varieties (miniature roses)
Selaginella spp. (moss fern)
Soleirolia soleirolii (baby's tears)
Strelitzia reginae (bird of paradise)

4

Stalking the Lazy Gardener's Plants

N ow that you have an idea of which plants to look for, where and how do you find reasonable plants? Apart from knowing which plants might be right for you, it helps if you use some finesse in shopping, and it will save you endless time and trouble if you begin by looking in the right places.

House-plant stores, florists, all-purpose garden centers, **where** suburban nurseries, supermarkets, some department **to look** stores, and five-and-ten-cent stores all stock house plants. The house-plant stores and garden centers are the best places to look for a wide selection of well-grown, healthy plants, particularly if you live in the city. If you can get to a suburban nursery, that might be even better, because this is where the city stores get most of their stock in the first place. You may not save money by buying directly from the nursery (they generally will charge the private customer the going retail price), but you will have a choice of all the plants there, instead of being limited to what the shopkeeper decides to bring into town.

Avoid mass-market, city-wide big chain plant stores, five-and-tens, chain-franchised operations in department stores, and supermarkets unless you happen to see a particular plant that you know is just right for you. Generally the quality of mass-market stock is uneven at best, and the staff cannot be particularly helpful because they are not trained plant people. As a rule, do not expect to find bargains in plants. Those on sale anywhere have generally been sitting in the store for too long and are in poor condition. They need extra work and special attention to restore them to good health, and extra work is just what you don't want. Five-and-tens and big chain plant stores usually keep their prices down, but you need a trained eye to sort out the good from the bad. The time and effort involved in wading through hundreds of plants just to find one or two healthy ones is probably not worth the saving, especially on small, relatively inexpensive plants.

There's no question about it; you will pay well for good plants from house-plant stores, garden centers, or nurseries, but these specialized places represent the trade. Most of their staff are people who have been working with plants for years. Their expertise can help you choose good plants and save you expensive mistakes. Some nurseries and garden centers and most house-plant stores stock pots, saucers, decorative containers, watering cans, and other plant accessories. The idea is to provide gardeners with one-stop shopping centers.

I've found that the small, individually owned and managed neighborhood plant stores are the easiest and most efficient to shop in. The very large plant stores depend heavily on a quick turnover of stock for their profits and tend to supply only those plants that are considered "best sellers." You can spend two hours going through a big store and see nothing but masses of dracaenas, philodendrons, asparagus ferns, and spider plants in three stock sizes—all very nice but there's a limit to how many six-foot dracaenas anyone wants in one home. The small "Mom and Pop store," most likely owned by a lifelong plant enthusiast, tends to go out on a limb and stock off-beat plants, even if they have to keep them for a while. You might see as many as a hundred different plants in a half-hour.

Even in the trade, some stores and nurseries are better than others. How can you tell? A good plant store, garden center, or nursery should be clean, well lighted, and appear to have its stock fairly well organized in terms of sizes and types of plants and plant accessories. It shouldn't be necessary to go from one end of the store to another to look at sixteen different small window-sill plants or poke around five sets of shelves to find a saucer to match a particular pot. In places where the plants are well cared for, the plants, pots, saucers, and planter trays will be clean and free of dust, fallen leaves, or other debris. Allowing for individual plant requirements, most plants should be freshly watered, and the store should have the faint fresh-earth scent of a garden after a spring rain. **what to look for in the store**

Most important, the plants should look perky and healthy with lush, typical growth. Be careful of any plant whose leaves appear distorted, too small, or off-colored. It could be that the plant in question is a different species than you think it is, and its appearance is entirely typical for that species. But if not, stunted or distorted growth indicates some weakness in the plant. If you buy it, you're off to a bad start even before you leave the store. In any case, avoid plants that appear wilted or shriveled or have faded or yellowing leaves, spots or cracks on the leaves, fine webs in the joints of leaves and branches or moving specks on the leaves—signs of insects. Check soil surfaces, bottoms of pots, and saucers for slugs, cockroaches, and earthworms, lest you wind up taking home some extra wildlife.

The Lazy Indoor Gardener

picking out the right plant No matter where you shop, you have to be fairly specific about your requirements. You now know something about growing conditions in your home, and you have lists of plants to choose from. Do not be discouraged if you think you're seeing the same kinds of plants in every store at one time. Plant stores depend on whatever they can get from their growers at any given time; if any particular plants seem to be unavailable everywhere, try again in a month or two.

Salespersons in plant stores can be helpful if you ask the right questions and make it quite clear that whatever you buy must be very easy to take care of and very adaptable and flexible in its requirements. However, the store is in business to sell plants. If you express great interest in a particular plant, you might wind up with some hopelessly fussy delicacy. It's no trick of salesmanship to persuade a customer to buy something he obviously wants.

In a good store you should be permitted to browse and look at everything. If something appeals to you, inquire about it casually or diffidently. Never ask if a plant is easy to grow. The salesperson will often reply, "Oh yes, it will grow anywhere, just needs a little water once a week," or some such spiel. It's much better to ask what the plant does need in the way of environment and care so you can decide if you are willing to accommodate those requirements. If neither you nor anyone in the store knows the name of a plant (botanical, as well as common), don't buy it. You can't very well research the care of a plant when you can't look it up because you don't know its name.

If you're shopping with certain plants in mind and you don't see them, ask for them. Good plant stores will often "special-order" a particular plant for you in a requested size if possible, or they might be able to help you find something else similiar in appearance and ease of care. If you can develop a good working relationship with one local store, stick with it. You'll benefit from such small, but useful, extra services as having your plants delivered, repotted if necessary, or special-ordered.

Finally, before you even leave your house, do have some idea of how much money you want to spend. It's incredibly easy to get carried away in a plant store. The energy crisis has had its adverse effect on the plant industry as well as everything else, and prices vary from one location to the next. However, to give you a general idea of cost: twenty dollars might buy five or six small plants (in two- to four-inch pots), three or four middling-sized plants (in five- or six-inch pots), two fairly large plants (in seven- or eight-inch pots), or, if it's something special such as a big cactus, possibly only one plant in a seven- or eight-inch pot. Hanging-basket plants usually run about twelve or fifteen dollars, and floor trees start at thirty or forty dollars, with top prices between a hundred and two hundred dollars.

5

Routine Plant Care

Common folklore has it that endless disasters befall house plants whose owners don't fuss over them like nervous mamas, play music for them, talk to them, pat them, and so on. The fact is that a lot of plants live in good condition for months on end without any attention whatever except watering.

Some plants—dracaenas, certain euphorbias, cacti, and philodendron, for example—will survive for a week or two with no water and no light. The last time I moved I brought two rosary vine plants along with me, and they spent an entire week inside a shopping bag. By the time I remembered that the plants were there, they were a bit wilted and the pots were quite dried out. I put them in the window and watered them, and in due time they recovered.

Assuming that plants and their environment are reasonably compatible, plant-keeping should be no more difficult or time-consuming than reading detective stories. In its way, plant-keeping can be just as relaxing.

Routine care does not involve anything more than watering and grooming. Even watering is not a daily chore and usually isn't necessary more often than two or three times a week.

watering No matter how frequently or infrequently a particular plant needs water, every watering has to be a thorough soaking. Pour the water slowly and evenly over the surface of the soil until it reaches the rim of the pot. Wait until it soaks in and see if there's any running out of the drainage hole in the pot. If so, you know that the entire root system and all the soil in the pot have been thoroughly moistened. If not, pour a little more water in until it starts trickling out of the drainage hole.

Once a plant receives a thorough watering, the pot should not stand in water; it's a house plant, not a rice paddy. Empty the overflow from saucers and plant trays. After you've watered a plant a few times, you'll have a good idea of how to give it a good soaking without causing an overflow all over the window sill.

Now that you've given your plant a good soaking, how can you tell when it's time to rewater? Plants should not be watered on any kind of regular time schedule, such as once a week, once a day, or every Friday and Monday. Instead, they should be grouped into three general patterns of watering: heavy, moderate, and light.

Heavy watering means that soil should be kept constantly damp, that is, towel-damp (the way a towel feels after you've just used it to dry your hair), not soggy wet. For moderate watering allow the soil to dry out thoroughly; then immediately rewater. Light watering means that soil should dry out completely and remain dry for several days before rewatering. Plants that require light watering, such as cacti and other succulents, aspidistra, and snake plant, are very good for people who travel frequently. The large specimens can remain dry for a week or two without suffering from lack of water.

Plants whose watering pattern is either moderate or light often collapse from overwatering. Gardeners fail to distinguish between soil that has really dried out since its last watering and soil that is still damp. The surface of the soil might look and feel dry, but underneath it might still be quite damp. Stick your finger into the soil about an inch in small pots, or two or three inches in large pots. If you can feel moisture below the surface, wait a day or two and finger-test again. If the soil feels quite dry below the sur-face, and the plant's watering pattern is moderate, rewater. If the plant has a light watering pattern, let the soil remain dry for several days. Plants, such as ivy and creeping fig, that require heavy watering should be watered again as soon as the surface of the soil feels dry.

Occasionally a plant appears to function for a month or two on a regular time schedule and seems to be ready for rewatering every four days or every week or whatever. Unfortunately, that convenient situation probably won't last. Seasonal changes and growth patterns can alter any plant's schedule. In spring and summer, when most plants are actively growing and their root systems are very thirsty, the soil dries out faster, so watering should be more frequent. In winter, when most plants are more or less dormant, the soil dries out more slowly. Damp weather and cool temperatures also slow down the drying-out process, but hot, dry summer weather or high indoor heat in winter speed it up. If plants are grown in air-condi-tioned rooms in summer, there might be no appreciable seasonal difference in their watering needs.

The soil in clay pots dries out faster than that in plas-tic pots of the same size. Plants in large pots dry out more slowly than those in small pots. Hanging pots of any size need more frequent watering than standing pots, because air circulates more around a hanging pot and also because heat rises.

Plant disasters that stem from watering problems usually come from overwatering rather than underwater-ing. If you forget or miscalculate by a day or two, or hap-pen to be away for the weekend just when a plant is ready to be rewatered, nothing disastrous will happen. At worst, the plant might wilt or droop slightly or even shed a leaf or two, but most plants can survive an occasional miss with

The Lazy Indoor Gardener

no great harm done. It's much worse if the soil and root system are not thoroughly moistened with each watering. Eventually roots that stay continuously dry (usually those at the bottom of the pot) wither away and the plant just topples over dead.

Overwatering is a common problem in indoor gardening. Either pots are allowed to sit in saucers full of water, or plants that should dry out completely between waterings are watered too soon, and the roots never have a chance to dry out. Eventually the roots rot away, and the plant sheds leaves or the leaves become soft and droopy, and finally the whole thing collapses altogether. If succulent plants, such as the jade plant, are overwatered, whole branches drop off until there's nothing left of the plant.

One more word about watering: A one-and-one-half quart watering can with a long, narrow spout is the most practical and efficient device for watering plants. It's not too heavy to manipulate when full, and it holds enough water to save you frequent refill trips. If you insist, you can use a juice jar, measuring cup, coffee pot, or dog-food can, but since this is the one plant chore you do regularly and often, you might as well use a tool designed for the purpose.

grooming Grooming can be considered a weekly event and, unlike watering, can be done to all the plants at once on any day convenient for you. Grooming includes misting, cleaning up dead leaves and other junk around the pots and saucers, picking dead leaves off the plant, and checking for insects and diseases. Such housekeeping chores are essential to prevent dead vegetation from attracting insects and disease organisms.

Misting involves spraying plants with clear cool water every other week and spraying with Cedoflora (sold in plant stores) or Dr. Bronner's Peppermint Castile Soap (available in health-food or some drug stores) on alternate weeks. Use a plastic one-pint mister bottle, which is the least expensive and most efficient tool. Spray enthusiastically over the entire plant, wetting down every leaf and branch. Be sure to hit the undersides of leaves and the joints of leaves and stems, since these are favorite hiding places for insects.

The point of the weekly misting is to dust off the plants and prevent insect invasions. Water alone might dislodge some insects, but Cedoflora or peppermint soap kills them. Either solution is a mild pest control, safe for all plants, safe to breathe or touch, safe to use around kids and pets (except fish tanks). These controls are effective for killing insects in the egg or larval stage when they are too small to be seen and before they do much damage. The biweekly spraying is a preventive measure that will nearly always check any insect invasion.

If humidity is very low or if any of your plants have suffered recently from insect ravages, then you should step up the misting program. Spray twice a week, once with clear water, once with Cedoflora or peppermint soap. Dilute Cedoflora in proportions of three teaspoons to a pint of cool water, and the peppermint soap in proportions of one-half tablespoon to a quart of cool water. The twice-weekly misting need only be continued for a month or so after an insect invasion.

Whenever you mist, look for signs of insects. Fine webs in the joints of leaves and stems or spread across leaves indicate spider mite. Black specks moving across leaves are aphids, and bits of cottony white fluff anywhere on the plant are mealybugs. Small pale-yellow specks that look like sesame seeds coating leaves are young white flies; the adults are unmistakable—they surround a plant in a great white cloud. Hard brown disks about one-eighth inch in diameter are scale insects. There are numerous other plant pests, but these are the most common. If you find insects in spite of buying clean plants to begin with and faithfully spraying them every week, there are several fairly simple remedies, described in Chapter 6.

Plants tend to grow toward the light source. During the weekly grooming session, rotate them in their places and with each other to prevent one-sided growth if some are closer to the light than others.

communing with plants Talking to (or at) plants, playing music for them, boosting up their morale, patting them, or stroking them won't hurt, but it won't help, either. A plant covered with mealybugs isn't going to get better if you send it a get-well card. Neither would you if you had scarlet fever and the doctor said "Have a drink, you'll feel better by morning!"

Plants require certain natural physical elements compatible with good growth; any psychological additives are merely anthropomorphisms. If it's true that plants react to human emotions and that they can feel shock and pain, then we should all stop cutting flowers, pruning trees, and eating vegetables. What are the vegetarians going to do?

6

Occasional Plant Care

Y our plants have been growing steadily for five or six months with no great effort on your part and, hopefully, few crises. Perhaps it's spring, and new leaves are burgeoning out on your ficus and your wrinkled cactus suddenly looks plump and round. Or maybe it's fall, and plants seem to be heaving out of their pots, and roots are beginning to trail out of drainage holes. It's time to fertilize and possibly repot. If some plants are taking up too much room because they've grown so well, you might want to cut them back a little. Here are a few ways for a lazy gardener to cope with these chores.

fertilizing

Plants need fertilizer to support active growth and to encourage the development of new leaves, roots, and flower buds. Not even the richest soil mixture supplies the extra nutrition provided by fertilizers that plants need while they're expending all that energy on bud and bloom. Plants lacking fertilizer might grow for a time, but they will not live as long, and growth is likely to be stunted or discolored.

Certain time-released fertilizers state on their labels that they are complete, balanced fertilizers. These are the only ones that lazy gardeners need to use. Follow instructions on the label—one application every six months is enough for most plants. Since the time-released fertilizer works slowly over months at a time, you can dispense forever with weekly, biweekly, or monthly fertilizing. The best months to do this chore are February or March, when plants begin to show new spring growth, and again in August or September, before plants have completed summer growth. Do not give a stronger dose than what the manufacturer recommends. Never fertilize before you go on vacation if a plant is ailing or when it is newly recuperating from repotting, neglect, insect invasions, or environmental change.

repotting   Plants that have been growing in the same soil for a year or more need repotting if they are to continue to grow vigorously. Even with fertilizing, plants use up the nutrients in their soil over a period of ten to twelve months if growth has been fairly steady, and need the nutritional boost of fresh soil.

If the soil seems to dry out within a day or less after a thorough watering, if the root system seems to be heaving out of the pot, or if bottom leaves drop off and new growth is stunted, the plants probably need to be transplanted or potted-on.

Strictly speaking, repotting means giving the plant fresh new soil and putting the plant back in the same pot or the same-sized pot. Moving the plant to a larger pot is called potting-on, or transplanting. Either repotting or potting-on should be an annual event for most plants, with the possible exception of very slow-growing cacti and most floor trees. Top-dressing (replacing surface soil) is the usual procedure for floor trees, especially if you prefer to keep them growing at a slow pace. It's also a much easier procedure for lazy people.

Advance planning saves you endless time and annoyance in repotting plants. Do all the shopping ahead of time—pots, soil, soil additives, hardware for hanging pots, and so on. You will need the next larger sizes for plants that have outgrown their pots, and enough soil materials to fill about half of each new pot. Old pots, scrubbed clean, can be recycled for new plants, or if they are cracked, hammered into small pieces and used for drainage material.

Some lazy gardeners prefer to have their local plant stores or plant doctors take care of repotting chores. For those of you who can summon up enough ambition to repot your own plants, here is a short discussion of materials and procedures.

pots

Pots and tubs made of clay, plastic, glazed pottery, acrylic, redwood, or pine—all with drainage holes—are your best choices for plant containers. Clay is porous, allowing water evaporation through the sides as well as the top of the pot, thus providing perfect moisture control. Succulent plants and plants with brittle, watery stems, such as impatiens and rex begonias, are best grown in clay pots because they speed up the drying-out process. If the top inch or two of soil in a clay pot feels dry, then you can be perfectly sure the soil has dried out all the way to the bottom—a good thing to know for any plant whose watering pattern is light or moderate.

Plastic, acrylic, and glazed pottery pots are less work to clean, and plastic and acrylic are also lightweight. However, water evaporation is slow, because these pots are not porous. That can be unhealthy for plants whose watering patterns are light or moderate, but very good for plants that need heavy watering. The nonporous pot helps to ensure constant dampness. Of the three kinds, I prefer the transparent acrylic pot because you can see water seeping down as you water and know when to stop. It spares the lazy gardener one more thought process. Also, you can see the soil gradually lighten in color as its drying occurs and know when it's time to rewater. Acrylic pots from five-and-ten stores are just as well made as and cheaper than those in plant or department stores.

Clay, plastic, and acrylic pots start at two and a half or three inches in diameter at the top of the pot and increase in size by one inch up to ten inches. Over ten inches, pot sizes graduate by two inches. Standard-height pots are as high as their top diameter; azalea pots are three-quarters the height of their diameter; and bulb pans are one-half as high as their top diameter. The type of pot you choose for each plant depends partly on how well the root system fits into that pot and whether the plant looks best in a tall or a shorter container.

Redwood and pine tubs (soya tubs from Taiwan) are available starting at nine inches in diameter. They are porous but less so than clay. If you're careful about finger-testing the soil before rewatering, then they can be used safely for any plant.

The same considerations regarding watering should be applied to the choice of plastic versus clay hanging pots. Any pot can be converted to a hanging pot with the many nylon, macramé, and rope hangers available in plant stores, five-and-tens, and department stores. Unless a plant is very full, it's better to avoid very elaborate hangers because they tend to dwarf the plant. Macramé, rope, and leather hangers sometimes rot away unnoticed at the point where they rest against the edges of the pot. Watch out for this after you've used such hangers for a while, lest you come home one day to find your hanging pot sprawled out all over the floor. Most hangers will accommodate pot and saucer, and some hanging pots are made with attached saucers.

Containers without drainage holes—baskets, jardinieres, bowls—should be used only as decorative covers for standard pots. Planting in holeless containers complicates

watering, and lazy gardening should not be more compli-
cated than necessary. Use decorative containers that are an
inch or two taller and two inches wider than the plant pots,
to allow air circulation and easy removal of the pots. Non-
waterproof decorative containers, such as baskets, should
be lined with either galvanized metal liners, which you can
have made if they are not sold that way, or several sheets
of heavy plastic. Put a one- or two-inch layer of pea gravel
or small stones at the bottom of these containers to provide
a drainage area for excess water. You can also set the pot
on a saucer inside the outer container. Be sure the saucer is
large enough to cover most of the bottom of the basket.

Plants in large pots usually don't need watering often
enough to make anyone feel like a slave to the watering
can. Plants in small clay pots might need more frequent
rewatering than you can handle. One way of getting
around this is to double-pot such plants. Set the plant in
another pot or decorative container that is larger by at least
two inches in diameter. Fill in all the extra space with
damp peat moss, which will slow down water evaporation
in the smaller pot.

soil The choice of soil mixtures varies from gardener to gardener, with everyone swearing to the efficacy of his particular favorite. Here are a few simple, effective mixtures
using readily available or store-bought materials. See
Chapter 3 for individual soil requirements for each plant.
These mixtures will accommodate all of the lazy gardener's plants.

For mixing soil with store-bought materials, you will
need packaged sandy soil (sometimes called cactus soil),
packaged humus, sharp sand (construction sand, not beach
sand), and Black Magic. Black Magic is an organic mixture
of peat, perlite, leafmold, wood chips, and other sub-
stances that contribute to plant nutrition and give a firm
texture to any soil mixture.

All-purpose soil mix: equal parts of sandy soil and Black Magic
Sandy soil mix: two parts sandy soil
two parts Black magic
one part sand
Humus soil mix: two parts sandy soil
two parts Black Magic
one part humus

For mixing soil with outdoor materials, you will need garden soil, leafmold (the rich, black soil that is found under trees or shrubs where fallen leaves have been allowed to decompose), peat moss, and sharp sand. Compost is an excellent substitute for leafmold.

All-purpose soil mix: two parts garden soil
one part leafmold or compost
one part peat
one part sand
Sandy soil mix: two parts garden soil
one part leafmold or compost
two parts sand
Humus soil mix: two parts garden soil
two parts peat
three parts leafmold or compost
one part sand

If your garden soil has just been turned and revitalized with the addition of peat, compost, and sand, you can use it for indoor plant mixtures in these proportions:

All-purpose soil mix: four parts soil to one part sand
Sandy soil mix: four parts soil to two parts sand
Humus soil mix: four parts soil to two parts compost

Outdoor materials are supposed to be sterilized to prevent weed seeds and soil-borne insects from making an appearance in your pots. Materials should be baked in a flat pan for an hour at 200 degrees. I'm too lazy to bother—besides, it makes my whole apartment smell like a peat bog. Luckily, my plants never have insects in the soil, and I have yet to grow a weed. I pick over outdoor soil with tweezers and remove the insects that I can see, if any.

Set aside one day for everything. Take the phone off the hook or keep it near you so you don't track soil all through the house running to answer it. Take everything you need outside, if possible, or spread newspapers thickly all over the kitchen floor. Let your kids watch and help, but chase the dogs and cats out of the room.

potting procedures

Water all plants to be repotted the night before or first thing in the morning. Potting is much simpler if plants are watered far enough ahead of time so that their soil and root systems have a chance to dry out slightly.

If you've never repotted plants, begin with the smallest ones. Otherwise, start with the largest ones to get the worst jobs over with.

Spread out your hand over as much as possible of the surface of the soil. Holding the bottom of the pot in your other hand—over the floor or kitchen counter—give it a sharp knock. Turn the pot upside down, and the plant should come out easily with root system and surrounding soil more or less intact. If not, bang again.

Occasionally a badly potbound plant will not slip out no matter how hard you bang. In that case, either break the pot by really hard knocking (but not so hard as to smash the root system), or work a table knife gently around the inside edges of the pot.

Now, look at the root system. Does it wind around the outer surface of the soil and appear to be rather massive? Good, the plant is growing well and needs a larger pot. If the root system seems to be practically solid, move the plant into a pot two sizes larger. Otherwise one size larger is sufficient. If the root system is still well covered with soil, then the plant can go back into the same-sized pot or the same pot.

To minimize disturbance to the roots, try to keep the root system and soil as intact as possible while you work. Of course, if you are just repotting the plant in fresh soil, you will have to shake or poke off some of the old soil to make room for the new. Work carefully and gently. If you do break some roots, cut back a corresponding amount of top growth, except with cactus plants.

Ideally, the new containers should be prepared before the plants are knocked out of their old pots, but this isn't always practical. If you're putting the plant back in the same pot, obviously you can't prepare it in advance. This would also be the case if you're putting one plant into a pot occupied at present by another plant.

In any case, keep the soil and root system damp, by covering it with several sheets of newspaper or plastic food wrap, while you prepare the new pot or clean the old. Scrub the pot and crock it. Crocking means using a few pieces of broken flowerpot to cover the drainage hole in a clay pot or putting a layer of pea gravel or small stones an inch or two deep in plastic pots.

New soil should be well dampened, but not soggy wet. Fill the pot about one third to one half full and spread the soil over the drainage layer and around the sides of the pot. Set the plant in the middle, and shake the pot gently so the new soil settles around the root system. Poke it down lightly with your fingers (or a pencil for very small pots) and add more soil if necessary to fill any space left. Water lightly. If the soil settles way down, add more until the surface is level all around. Water lightly again, and put the plant back in its usual place, unless that place is very sunny. Newly repotted plants are best kept out of full sun for the first few days.

There are three important things to remember about repotting. First, if you have to stop in the middle of everything, keep the root system damp. If it's necessary to leave the plant out of the pot overnight, wrap the roots in soil and enclose roots and soil in a plastic bag. Second, the soil line on the plant must be the same as it was when the plant was in the old pot. The soil line is the point on the stem or stems where the soil stops and the plant emerges above ground. You can tell that point by the color of the stem—the part above ground is lighter than the part below ground. Third, once a plant is settled into its new pot, there should be enough space between the surface of the soil and the top of the pot for watering—about a half-inch in small pots and one to one and a half inches in pots over five inches in diameter.

If plants seem to droop after repotting, keep them enclosed in plastic bags punched with a few holes. Some plants, especially those that need heavy watering, suffer a mild and temporary culture shock from repotting. The plastic bag serves as a sort of protective, high-humidity recovery room.

If floor trees and cacti are not obviously falling out of their pots, and if they have been in their pots for less than two years, top-dressing is sufficient for their needs and is a simple procedure. Using a kitchen fork, gently scratch out the top inch or two of soil, being careful not to disturb the little roots near the surface. Replace what you have removed with fresh new soil, and lightly water it in. That's all; your big plant is set for another year.

Despite the lazy gardener's well-meant if least strenuous **pruning** efforts, vining plants and sometimes shrubby or treelike plants occasionally get out of hand, particularly if their environment is very good. Like bedmates who hog the blankets, such plants grab half the room on the window sill and block out much of the light for slower-growing plants. Cut them back. Use a sharp kitchen knife and cut just below the joints of leaves and stems at whatever point you want the growth to be arrested. Since you've temporarily halted growth, do not fertilize until the plant puts out new growth.

Cutting back is a good way of encouraging bushy growth on plants that tend to grow long and leggy or skimpy and trailing. Rosary vine, philodendron, grape ivy, coleus, impatiens, ficus, myrtle, avocado, wandering Jew, and other shrubby or vining plants respond very well to annual spring pruning. If the plant is not overly large, do not cut it back, but merely pinch off the growing tips with your first fingernail and thumbnail.

Slicing off part of a cactus encourages new growth. For every piece you cut off, two will usually grow in its place.

training Vines can also be trained to frame a window sill. Tack a string around the window frame or wherever you would like the vine to go, and tie the vine to the string with plastic-coated wire at various inconspicuous points several inches apart. You can also train a vine to wrap itself around a wire coat hanger bent into shape, a stake, or a piece of tree bark.

Repot the plant, and plant the hanger or whatever you use along with it. Take the longest strands of the vine and wrap them around the hanger, tying them in various places if necessary. Eventually the plant will grow along the trainer more or less on its own. Leave the shorter strands of the vine to trail over the sides of the pot. *Hoya bella, hoya carnosa* (wax plant), grape ivy, and pothos will wrap themselves around anything.

making new plants If, lazy or not, you can't bear to throw out all those pieces you've just cut off your overgrown plants, here are two simple ways of starting new plants from any pieces over five or six inches long.

First, fill a four-inch pot about half full with soil. Allowing room for watering on top, fill the rest of the pot with a mixture of half sand or perlite and half peat moss, thoroughly dampened. Snip each cutting to a point just below the joint of a leaf and stem, and pick off the bottom leaves of the first three or four joints. Poke holes in the sand and peat layer with a thin, long nail and insert the cuttings. The sand and peat layer should cover the bottom three or four joints; if not, angle the cuttings on their sides and pin down with a paper clip or hairpin. Cover pot and cuttings with a plastic bag punched with a few holes, and put in a shady window.

Another method is to prepare the cuttings as directed above and to insert them into Jiffy-7 pots. These are little peat blocks enclosed in plastic netting. They can be set in a muffin tin and covered with a plastic bag. Jiffy-7 pots are available in plant stores and five-and-ten stores.

Both methods are based on the principle that the cuttings will root at the joints of leaves and stems. While the roots are in the first, tender stages of growth, they will be growing in the sterile medium of sand and peat or Jiffy pots. When the roots are more developed, they will grow right into their natural soil. If you use Jiffy pots alone, move the plant and pot intact into a regular pot filled with soil when the roots start poking through the plastic netting.

In both methods, keep all planted materials thoroughly dampened. When the cuttings show signs of new growth, move them into a light window and open the plastic bags at the top, but do not remove the bags for another week. This helps the new plants gradually adjust to the reduced humidity outside the plastic bag. Check every so often to see that the pots are still damp.

Leave the plastic bags open at the top from the start for plants such as impatiens and coleus that have brittle, watery stems. These cuttings need some extra humidity but not as much as they get in a closed plastic bag.

Cacti and succulents are very easily multiplied. Very small leaves will root and produce new plants if they are simply left on the surface of the soil. Larger pieces should be sliced at the bottom so that they have a flat edge. Sear the flat edge with an iron set on "synthetic," and poke the cutting just below the surface of the soil. Keep the soil barely damp, and leave the pot in a sunny window.

A light dusting of rooting powder, called Rootone, around the bottoms of cuttings will speed up rooting, but it isn't absolutely necessary.

pest control If, during your weekly grooming session, you find signs of insects, the simplest remedy for the lazy gardener is to throw the plant out. Certainly, if the plant is badly afflicted (insects on more than a third of the plant for instance), it isn't worth anyone's time and effort to save it. It's probably already so weakened, it will never recover. If many leaves have already turned yellow, fallen off, curled up, are torn or chewed, or coated with a sticky substance, the plant has had it.

If the plant appears to be fairly intact and you see just a few signs of insects, then it's worth operating on. First, remove the plant from its neighbors and spray heavily with Cedoflora. Be sure to get the undersides of the leaves. Keep the afflicted plant away from any other plants and spray daily until you are sure there are no more insects. You can even spray twice daily—once with cold water, once with Cedoflora.

Check all the other plants very closely, particularly those adjacent to the afflicted plant, and treat them as above if you find others with insects. If not, institute the twice-spraying program.

Spraying with Cedoflora should take care of early insect invasions. Admittedly, daily spraying might seem to be a nuisance to a lazy person, but it is much less of a bother than using strong, toxic insecticides. After a week of this routine, if the plant is still not "cured," try spraying with Malathion. This is the one strong insecticide that is acceptable, if used with care, to ecologists and environmentalists. Its residual effects are short-lived, and except in very strong doses it is evidently not toxic by inhalation or skin contact. Nevertheless, spray outdoors, if possible, pointing the spray downwind so that you inhale as little as possible. In the city, outdoors can be the roof of your building, the fire escape, or even the stoop. When it's necessary to spray in winter, the plant won't collapse if you take it outside just long enough to spray.

If you can't spray outdoors, at least do it in a well-ventilated room from which you have removed fish tanks, birds, cats, dogs, and kids. Malathion smells awful, but the odor will dissipate in an hour or so. If you get any on your skin or clothes, take a shower and throw your clothes in the wash. Follow directions on the bottle for diluting, and mix only enough for one application. Once diluted, Malathion doesn't keep. Repeat twice at weekly intervals. If that doesn't work, throw the plant out.

Malathion and Cedoflora can also be used as dips. For very small plants (those you can lift with one hand), cover the soil with tin foil and hold it in place with one hand. Turn the pot over and dip the whole plant in the insecticide solution. For very large plants, for which spraying might involve spraying half the room, paint the solution on with a two- or three-inch paintbrush. Be sure to "paint" all parts of the plant.

Root and/or soil-borne pests, such as nematodes (worms) and pot and saucer pests (ants, slugs, black flies, cockroaches, and moths), are not overly difficult for lazy gardeners to eradicate. Soil pests are obviously not visible unless you take the plant out of its pot and look at the roots. If you potted the plant in sterilized (store-bought) soil, you probably won't ever get nematodes. If the plant is ailing and you've eliminated all obvious causes, unpot the plant and examine the soil and roots. If you see small wormy things crawling around or hanging on to the roots, either throw away the plant and soil or wash off roots under a slow faucet in warm water. Repot in store-bought soil and, for good measure, pour in a solution of Malathion.

Moths and black flies are not a plant problem themselves, but some lay eggs in the soil that become plant-eating larvae. Ants do not harm plants, either, but they attract other insects and actually carry them around from plant to plant. Cockroaches and slugs eat plants, and roaches lay their eggs in the soil.

When you see any of these crawling or flying insects hovering over the plants or crawling around pots and saucers, drench the soil with Malathion. Get rid of the insects with Cedoflora or peppermint oil laced with rubbing alcohol or 100-proof distilled spirits. Do not spray plants with the alcoholic solution; plants do not like alcohol. If crawling insects persist, drench the soil monthly with one-half tablespoon of Pine-Sol (a household cleaner) diluted in a pint of water.

Disease organisms, which produce leaf spots, rotting stems and leaves, and mold, sometimes infect indoor plants. Diseases are usually caused by extremely high or low temperatures, insects, overwatering, or excess humidity. If the plant is badly affected, throw it out. Otherwise, pick off affected leaves and stems and correct for environmental problems and insects. If the difficulty persists, apply Benlate, an organic, systemic fungicide, to the soil.

That, I think, is as much as any lazy or casual gardener wants to do about plant pests. Most other insecticide solutions and aerosol sprays are ecologically undesirable for one reason or another, and the precautions you must take in order to use them safely make the whole project entirely too much bother.

vacation care

Here are several suggestions for keeping your plants healthy while you are away. Having someone look after the plants while you're gone is the easiest. Failing that, I've found that the simplest procedure is to water every plant and wrap the pots with plastic food wrap covering as much of the soil as possible. Unless the vacation is to be more than two weeks long, wrapping pots of cacti or very large floor trees isn't necessary. For plants that need to be constantly damp—especially creeping fig, Boston fern, and ivy—covering the plant and pot with a plastic bag, as well as wrapping the pot, is a good idea. Punch a few holes in the bag to ensure ventilation.

To guard against possible pest invasion, especially if the plants have been recently affected, water the soil with a Pine-Sol solution and spray top growth with Cedoflora.

Do not fertilize before you go away. Also, pick off flower and leaf buds. Move plants in very light windows slightly away from the windows, especially if they are under plastic bags. The idea is to slow down growth in order to reduce the need for frequent watering.

7

Further Strategies of Lazy Gardening

Speaking in theatrical terms, plant care should be light entertainment, not a heavy drama. You are supposed to enjoy your plants, not be overwhelmed by them. The following are some of the more esoteric strategies that help keep everything light and lend cachet to a plant collection.

�֎ The plant doctor, who is not always a horticulturist but is a person with great practical expertise in house plants, can be very useful for certain purposes. Plant-doctor services run high, as much as twenty-five dollars an hour, but for regular work or major jobs you should be able to work out something reasonable.

Using a plant doctor is the most efficient solution for keeping your plants alive and well during your vacation and traveling absences. He waters, fertilizes, cleans up, and treats ailments. You return from your travels to find all your plants in peak condition. A variation of this arrangement is to rent your apartment or house during your absence to someone who knows how to take care of plants and will look after them.

If the annual chore of repotting, transplanting, and pruning all your plants gives you a headache just thinking about it, call the plant doctor. He can do the whole job in a day or two while you go to work or take in a good movie.

Be sure that your arrangement with him includes his cleaning up all the mess.

The plant doctor can bail you out in times of crisis. If your plants are ailing and you can't figure out what's wrong, let him diagnose and treat the plants accordingly. You will be saved the bother of spraying, drenching, and repotting. Plant doctors advertise their services in local weekly newspapers. Your friendly neighborhood plant store might be able to help you find one.

✖✖ If a plant doctor is unavailable or too expensive, trade off vacation-time watering chores with a friend or neighbor. Share the repotting chores. Invite one or two plant people for an old-clothes Saturday lunch or Sunday brunch in the spring or fall when most plants need repotting. Take all the plants and repotting materials, along with cold drinks, up to the roof or outside, and repot, prune, transplant, whatever. The chores will go faster and seem less tedious, and if you can do the work outdoors, cleaning up is minimized. Afterwards, wash up, then sit down and enjoy your lunch.

✖✖ Plants are not static objects. They grow, leaf out, trail, climb, bloom, and so on. If any of yours seem to just sit in one place and do nothing, perhaps your growing environment is not good for them. In any case, when a plant seems to go nowhere, you'll soon be bored with it and even less motivated to take care of it. Find a friend with plants that you like which might grow more successfully in your house, and see if you can work out a trade.

✖✖ Send your plants to summer camp. Find someone with a garden, patio, or backyard who wouldn't mind having some bare spots filled in with potted plants, and who will be home during the summer to hose down your plants along with his own. The plants benefit tremendously from a summer outdoors, and you can trip off to the beach every weekend without worrying about plant sitters. At the end of the summer, call the plant doctor for a repotting session—your plants will be jumping out of their pots.

❈ Concentrate your plant collection on big plants. A few floor trees and/or massive hanging baskets are much showier than lots of little pots, cost no more to buy, and are easier to tend. Bonuses of large plant collections include much less frequent watering, because the big pots dry out slowly, and reduced plant mortality, because older plants become more disease- and bug-resistant.

❈ Focus on two or three different kinds of plants, buy them in many different sizes, and pot them in a variety of pots and decorative containers. My neighbors upstairs do this with spider plants in hanging pots and various dracaena species standing on the floor. The pots and jardinieres are all beautiful one-of-a-kind, handmade pottery containers, and the plants become sculptural shapes accenting a magnificent pot collection. Across the way, my other neighbors achieve the same dramatic effect with grape ivy in hanging baskets and schefflera and podocarpus on the floor. Their containers consist of baskets collected in their travels, from auctions, off-beat stores, the five-and-ten, sometimes on the street. With only two or three sturdy, undemanding species of plants to look after, plant chores are minimal.

❈ If you find that one particular plant species seems to do especially well for you, collect all its relatives, as many as you can find in that particular plant family. With high light, a desert cacti collection is the easiest group of plants to grow. Usually, most plants in one family have similiar cultural requirements. When you become a specialist, and limit your collection to one plant type, your chores are greatly simplified.

❀ Let one window be your garden window, and put all your plants there. Chores will be greatly simplified if all the plants are collected in one place and you don't have to wander from room to room and window to window dribbling the watering can all over the furniture.

❀ If you have several very small plants, such as cacti, cluster them inside one basket or inside one jardiniere. They look more interesting gathered together than lined up side by side, and watering is easier because you have one big container catching all the drip instead of several little saucers with water sloshing out of them.

❀ Are your window sills too shallow for large plants? To extend a window sill, cut an eight- or ten-inch shelf board to fit the length and interior configuration of the existing window sill. Nail or screw it into the window sill. Then reinforce it with right-angle irons screwed into the board and up the side of the window frame or shelf brackets screwed into the wall below the window sill and under the overhang. Paint or stain the new window sill to match the window frame.

If radiator heat under a window is a problem use this extended window sill as a buffer zone by raising it on one-by-two-inch boards.

❀ Buy the prettiest, functional watering can that you can find and set it in a conspicuous place near the plants. When pretty tools are on display, it's more fun to use them for chores.

❀ If your plant collection is small and looks skimpy, show it off with a collection of statuary or small art objects. One collection enhances the other, and you don't have to water the statuary.

✖ Turn recessed windows into greenhouses by enclos-
ing the area with glass or plexiglass shades or doors. If hot,
dry room air defeats all your attempts to grow anything,
the enclosure will protect plants by keeping temperatures
down and humidity up. Pots will dry out much more
slowly, and the glass doors allow easy access and easy
viewing.

✖ Pot all your plants in the same kind of pot (all clay or
all acrylic, for example) with matching saucers, or set all
pots into one style of basket or jardiniere. This is purely
for psychological effect. It does not change the fact that you
have all those plants to look after, but it makes the job
seem manageable because the plants look organized!

✖ Seasonal flowering plants give color and novelty to the
"basic green" foliage plant collection, last much longer
than cut flowers, and are correspondingly less expensive.
You don't have to do anything to them except picking off
dead blooms and watering them. Seasonal potted flowers
include poinsettias and Christmas cactus at Christmas;
forced tulips, hyacinths, and narcissus during the winter,
especially around Valentine's Day; lilies, begonias, cin-
erarias, cyclamen, and azaleas around Easter and Mother's
Day; annuals, such as marigolds, petunias, alyssum, zin-
nias, ageratum, lobelias, and impatiens, from May through
the summer; chrysanthemums in the fall.

Keep potted flowers in full bloom away from the sun,
but give plants in the budding stage as much sun as possible to encourage bloom. Annuals, chrysanthemums, and
begonias will be encouraged to bloom a second time if
dead flowers are snipped regularly. Watering for all potted
flowers should be heavy. Chrysanthemums, azaleas, begonias, and impatiens can be transplanted outdoors if you
have a garden. If this isn't possible, discard plants after
blooming.

Try displaying four or five small pots of different annuals or bulb flowers inside a basket with a saucer at the bottom. The basket of flowers can be moved to the dinner or coffee table and will last much longer than a bouquet of cut flowers for the same price.

❊ If potted flowers are unavailable, add "instant flowers" to foliage plants by using cut flowers. Snip stems fairly short and poke them gently into the soil in and around the branches of freshly watered low-growing or vining plants, such as pothos, philodendron, creeping fig, baby's tears, or asparagus fern. If you've just spent a half-day's pay on a bouquet of flowers for a centerpiece and they look like nothing, this is a good way to beef them up into a nice display.

❊ If a plant you like in a store comes only in small sizes and you want a big one, buy two or three small ones and have the store repot them in a larger pot with suitable soil. Check all potted plants before you buy them to see if they are imminently in need of repotting, in which case have the store do it before you take them home. The extra service charge, if any, is worth it. You won't have to think about repotting those plants for another year and the mess of repotting will be in the store, not your kitchen.

❊ Invest in three plastic mister bottles—one for misting with clear water, one for spraying Cedoflora or peppermint soap, and one for spraying with Malathion. That way, you don't have to bother rinsing out one substance thoroughly before using the same bottle for another solution.

❊ Is misting near your windows a problem because of non-water-resistant curtains? Collect all the plants you can lift on a tea wagon or other portable tray and wheel them into the bathroom. Spray, wheel them back, and return them to their usual places. Floor plants can be moved if they are set on platforms with casters, which can be found at garden centers, or on movers' dollies. You can make your own platform by screwing casters into three-quarter-inch plywood boards. Paint or stain the dollies or plywood to match the pots. Movable plants simplify vacuuming, window-cleaning, and other housekeeping chores and can be easily transported to other places in the house for temporary decorative effect.

❀ Would your very high ceilings look nice with hanging plants at different levels? Hang them on pulley ropes or weighted chains, which you can pull down for watering and raise again.

❀ If you don't use decorative containers, stand all your plants on one large tray filled with pebbles. Mount the hanging plants above the plants standing in this tray. Watering is much simpler if one tray collects all the drip and you don't have a whole lot of saucers to keep clean and drain the overflow from. You can make or have made galvanized metal trays to fit window sills or, for floor trees, shallow plywood boxes treated with cuprinol and lined with galvanized metal.

❀ Automatic watering gadgets, homemade and otherwise, seem to be sprouting up everywhere. One type is a small bulb with a clay nipple. The nipple is inserted into the surface of the soil and the bulb filled with water. As the soil dries out, the bulb releases more water into the soil. Another device consists of a bowl with several curved wicks. One end of a wick rests in the bowl, which is filled with water, and the other end is poked into the soil. The wicks gradually draw water from the bowl into the soil as the soil dries out.

Another automatic waterer is a self-watering pot. This is basically a small pot with plant and soil set into a larger pot which holds a reservoir of several weeks' supply of water. These self-watering pots only come in small sizes, probably because it's the small plants that need the most frequent watering.

The advantage of these gadgets is that you simply fill the part of the device that holds water and you don't have to decide whether the plant needs water. However, at three dollars apiece they are expensive if you have a lot of plants. You might find them worthwhile if you travel frequently or take long vacations, especially if plant sitters turn out to be even more expensive.

A homemade wick waterer is simple and inexpensive to make. Take five or six inches of quarter-inch-width clothesline, and fray an inch or two at one end. Poke the frayed end into the drainage hole at the bottom of an empty plant pot. Then pot the plant as usual *without crocking or other drainage material.* Set the pot on pebbles, or anything that will hold it up, inside a watertight container that is several inches taller than the pot. Fill the container with water to the point where it doesn't quite touch the bottom of the pot. The remaining three or four inches of clothesline dangling out of the drainage hole in the pot should trail in the water and will draw water into the soil as the soil dries out.

A less elegant version of the wick waterer is a shoelace with one end poked deep into the soil of a pot and the other end dangling in a jar of water next to the pot. Both devices work for plants collected on one big tray. Just fill the tray with water, making sure that the pots are not sitting below the water line. Let the wicks dangle in the tray.

The major drawback of all automatic waterers is that they can only be used for plants that require heavy watering, in other words, plants that should stay damp at all times. The watering gadget does not distinguish between your creeping fig, which should never dry out, and your hedgehog cactus, which must dry out and stay dry for a while before rewatering. For occasional brief vacations, you can safely use an automatic waterer for any plant,

although you would need a laundry tub to supply a sufficient reservoir of water for large plants.

If you do use automatic waterers regularly, the plants
should be potted in sandy soil and well crocked to ensure
perfect drainage.

❁ Have you ever read about gypsies or farmers whose
services were highly sought after by well-diggers because
they were believed to have some mystical power of divin-
ing water under the surface of apparently arid land? You
can be your own water-diviner with one or two gadgets
that tell you whether your plants need to be watered, that
is, if the soil has really dried out all the way to the bottom
of the pot. One type is a device that you stick into the
surface of the soil and leave there. When it changes color,
it's time to water. Another gadget is a hand-held numerical
water meter with a cable and metal probe. Stick the probe
deep into the pot, and the moisture content of the soil will
register on the meter. The disadvantage is that poking any
mechanical device into the soil can damage plant roots.
The best gadget for measuring water is a water meter that
registers wet, moist, or dry, and is attached to a simple
straight probe designed to minimize damage to plant roots.

I still think that one's fingers are entirely reliable indi-
cators for determining whether a plant needs to be watered, but you might enjoy the precision qualities of these
horticultural devices.

❁ Protect window sills and provide a buffer zone for
plants set on top of radiators by using bricks. No construction is necessary, and you can arrange the bricks in layers,
setting some of the trailing plants on higher levels. The
bricks take care of the problem of dirt and water damage
on window sills. Plants, clay pots, and bricks, especially
old bricks, have a natural affinity for one another. Natural-
colored baskets and soya tubs also look well with bricks.

About the Author

ROBERTA PLINER is a New York-based writer who learned everything she knows about lazy indoor gardening from growing many different kinds of plants, with as little work as possible, in a Manhattan apartment. She is the co-author of *Rx for Ailing House Plants* and *The Terrarium Book*.